M000277787

WHAT JUST HAPPENED

STORIES IN VERSE

WHAT JUST HAPPENED

STORIES IN VERSE

Barbara Baillet Moran

Published by

BONVENTURA PRESS

Copyright 2021 by Barbara Baillet Moran
All rights reserved.

No part of this book may be reproduced or
transmitted in any form or by any means
without written permission from the publisher.

Book design by Scott Davis

Cover photograph by Colin Moran
Author photograph by Kathryn Moran

Published by
Bonventura Press
Aspen, Colorado, U.S.A.
WhatJustHappenedBook@gmail.com

ISBN 978-0-578-87591-0

Library of Congress Control Number: 2021905033

for Bill Moran
without whom much that happened
would not have

The only end of writing is to enable readers
better to enjoy life, or better to endure it.

SAMUEL JOHNSON

CONTENTS

III. BEYOND THE BURROW

IV. ALL FALL DOWN

V. NOT JUST ABOUT THE FOOD

VI. NOT DIGNIFIED

VII. BOUQUETS

VIII. GRANDCHILDREN

PREFACE

Thirty years ago, memories began to emerge in my nightmind—that dusky state muses visit. They arrived in the form of anecdotes, portraits, vignettes, conversations—materials later woven into poems and stories featuring dialogue I could not have invented.

An earlier book of social history was painstakingly planned. Now, without specific intention, I was gradually setting down an informal autobiography, beginning with a child's perceptions of World War II, concluding with the reflections of an octogenarian.

During those years, I often wondered just what was happening—the world seemed to spin ever faster and more malignantly. I was drawn to add contemporary question, observation, rumination, fantasy to the growing collection.

As I attempted to assemble this composite brew, I was pleasantly surprised to discover that the writing fell naturally into ten chapters: Life and its subtopics.

Years ago, I studied with the great Appalachian storyteller Don Davis, whose stories invariably made listeners laugh, then cry. Often asked if his stories were true, he would reply, "They have truth in them."

Writing these pieces over many years, I gradually became bolder, took more risks. Thus, wordplay, puns, extreme alliteration, singing rhymes, invented words, general frothiness seemed appropriate for wild, improbable times. Still, the Davis maxim remained a lodestar. As did his porous boundaries between laughter and tears.

Much was written in the third person—an attempt to draw attention away from the writer and toward the story. Like most writers, I hope that my particulars will be universals for others.

I ask the reader's indulgence for my occasional use of Latin words. Late in life, my husband and I found the Latin Tridentine Mass beautiful and deeply affecting (as we had not in childhood). Certain profound phrases called out to serve.

The cover photograph was taken in the Colorado Rockies, where two of our sons live. The ten trees in the picture symbolize for me our ten family members and the landscape we revere.

At another level, the apparent mist at the photograph's center suggests the ambiguity of this collection's title. What just happened here—snowfall, misty rain, a drifting cloud, or smoke from forest fires?

As do many books, this one gradually chose its own nature. Most of the writing is from one life but evolved to speak of many lives. If these tales alert, console, stir emotion or simply entertain, then I will deem that active nightmind absolved for years of sleep invasion.

Barbara Baillet Moran
Greensboro, N.C.
2021

I

MORNING

My Father's War, 1944

Some nights, we heard only soft rain,
then the fluttering shudder
of his rubber slicker
shaken out in the vestibule.

Three children making him ineligible
for the draft, my father, volunteer fireman
and air-raid warden, sounded the siren.
Night drills—lights out, curtains drawn, all still.

Too young to ask why Mother was tense,
we children huddled inside, waited
serenely. Dad was in charge,
would keep us all safe.

Finally, the all-clear; his siren wailed
again—relief, lights, cocoa.
Our father had taken care
of Everything.

1949

Winters on the island were colder then.
Thick pond ice held dozens of skaters.
Children took skates to school,
and at the bell raced
to the pond for the hour
before darkness descended.

We sat on logs, laced up, dashed off.
Older boys raced ruddy-faced
down the straight-away,
girls gathered in talk-skate groups.
First-graders struggled for traction,
ankles buckling, adults absent, no offer
of a mittened hand. Older skaters, minding
the brutal code of youth, ignored the sprawlen:
all must pay icy dues.

And pay we did, we thought,
if we thought at all, on the long dark trudge
home, cherry noses, fingers and toes
close to frostbite, still enchanted by
our pond, our woods, our silver sky.

Fallible

Long ago, Aunt Reine would say,
A child your age should know Aesop.
or *You've never heard of De Gaulle?*

I was, in fact, a mildly precocious little beast,
devouring the weekly *Life* and *Time* at eight,
The Sunday Times at twelve, *Webster's*
in spare moments.

Not enough. Alas, I could not learn
everything. Aunt plucked out weakness.
Surely, you've read Jane Austen by now?

Years later, with Reine not so tall,
I, now grown, observed over tea,
Look, Auntie—on the plate—
just like a Proust madeleine!

What, my dear, is a madeleine?

You remember—the cookie that unlocked
Proust's memories.

I have no idea what you're talking about.

Puzzled, I exclaimed, *But I grew up
with your French!*

Then, God forgive me,
Surely Auntie, you've read Proust by now.

Reine's face burned as she turned away.
I relive the moment without pleasure, only shame.
Weakness surprises with its many guises,
keeps us tame.

Awakening

At twelve, she was chosen.
The sole child
with four adults, offered
an evening of dinner
and the New York City Ballet.

The fine food and conversation
directed to *her*—as enthralling
as the ballet. Alas, she nodded off—
a school night after all.
Alert again on the long drive home,
she heard the word *intelligentsia*,
knew she was in its company,
the word, the night to be enshrined
in her childmind.
Uncertain about the word's exact meaning,
yet she knew. *This must be my life.*
Once chosen, now she would choose.

Recalling heated discussions
hosted by her parents, she asked,
Mom, are you and Dad of the intelligentsia?
Puzzled, amused, her mother smiled,
No dear, why do you ask?
Ah, why indeed . . . ?

Mother's Gentleman Caller

Mother's friend arrived in mid-afternoon,
just as we children returned from school.
Was it once a month, or once a week,
I cannot recall; always welcome
in our lives, not unusual or unseemly,
Mr. Levine, later Uncle Maurice,
in a herringbone worsted, vested suit
taught mathematics and smoked cigars.

His words, sensible and wise,
offered in precise diction,
matched his sartorial grace.
Clouds of pungent smoke wreathed
our exotic guest,
perfumed the afternoons.

A kind teacher years before,
asked a student to stay,
seeing perhaps, a precious stone
in need of polish, setting, display.

They drank iced tea in summer heat;
on winter days, light of mood,
Mother served sweet wine
with slices of cake and tea,
daring for the place and time.

In that innocent day,
fires were banked, dusk scented
with Monte Cristos, sherry and tokay.

Bread and Steel

On Long Island, the post-war years,
Mr. Kreutzer's accent was familiar to her.
She knew children whose parents
fled Kristallnacht.

On Sunday mornings, long lines
formed outside his small bakery.
Her first job, age fifteen,
was to box and ring up
three prune, two cherry,
one apple Danish, two seeded rye sliced,
a pumpernickel, four hard rolls—and fast.
Cheerful, chattering, the after-church
crowd was patient but eager
for the unrivaled goods
of the lean man working quietly
in the back room,
hands dusted in flour.

His day began at three; working alone
he baked for the army
soon to crowd his door.
By noon on Sundays, six on weekdays,
shelves were empty, cash register full.

She swept floors, soaked pans, while
he scrubbed ovens, washed steel counters.
An incurious adolescent, she did not think
to ask why he grimaced when lifting
iron pots, stacks of metal trays.

Amidst clean and gleaming surfaces
in the dim light of the back room,
polished tools glowing in corners,
he would sit down at last,
drink coffee, eat a roll.

Exhausted, he would talk, recall
the village of his childhood,
how he learned to bake.

A sweet, tranquil bond grew.
Shrapnel, he said one day.
Dozens of little pieces—can't be removed.
That's why I'm so slow.

Slow? Hardly, she thought.
You were a soldier?
She paused as the shaft penetrated.
For the Germans?
Her uncle had been wounded
in the war, a neighbor killed.

Her languid mind struggled
with this first knowledge.
He was a good man.
Still,
the gentle baker's hands
had not always been covered
in flour.

This story from over sixty years ago was recalled after conversations with a gentle friend who practiced medicine into his 80s. Born in Germany, Xaver was conscripted into the German army at seventeen after an anti-Hitler letter he wrote was intercepted by the secret police. Had his father not been widely respected, Xaver would have been shot. Instead, he was sent to battle. His handsome face bears scars from wounds received at Stalingrad. Dr. Hertle and his late wife Marianne moved to the U.S. in 1956 and were active, civic-minded American citizens for the rest of their lives.

Haunted

We met
on the first weekend
of my blind-date-splattered
college career.
Herd met herd, as arranged
by well-meaning counselors.
After all the bumping and jostling,
elbowing toward
this gleam of yellow hair,
that undulation under pink cashmere,
after hanging back from the fray,
unsure of how this was all supposed
to work, (how did they all know it was
a first-come, first-served market?)
there you were, standing alone.

You were small, frail.
Thin hair too, dark and lank.
Thick spectacles, of course,
—harbingers of your future
on Park Avenue—but few knew
or cared what lay beyond
that prescription glass.

Decency forbids description of your complexion.
Suffice to say, science was as yet unable
to unblight your adolescence.
You were indeed ill at ease, well aware
of the robust health, radiant beauty
against which you were judged.

I did not, could not, offer comfort. A hint
of good will, a small joke, if mirthless?
Beyond me—for an entire evening.
Rueful comments on the shared lot
of greenhorns everywhere?
No. I had nothing to give you.
An injured silence. That was all.
I never saw you again.

Ten, perhaps twenty, years later
you began to inhabit my dreams,
a reminder of how to live,
and how not to . . .
You will haunt me forever.

English Saddle and a Fifth of Scotch

They were college freshmen,
partners in biology lab.
He nurtured a knowing manner,
had answers—so *he* thought—
to questions she had just
begun to formulate.

He seemed decent enough.
She learned as quickly as he,
navigated collegiate corridors
as well as he—*she* thought.

So why, she wondered,
the odd, impersonal manner,
the lofty style?
(the word *entitled* not yet in vogue).

After Christmas, new sophisticates
still enquired about gifts received.
His casual reply, *A fifth of scotch
from Father,
An English saddle from Mother.*

Thus began her true education.

Invitations

She had read Hemingway, Fitzgerald,
even a bit of Gertrude Stein.
So she knew Cambridge in 1960,
still the fifties, after all,
was to be her Paris.

Gray clapboard facade, four walk-ups,
wooden fire escapes, a few blocks
from Harvard Square,
a dozen bright young things—
law students, a veteran or two,
four fresh-faced Ivy alums.

Open doors and communal meals,
late nights of music, cigarettes, coffee,
debate, gesticulation, finely-tuned
definitions (some schooled by Jesuits).
No television, endless talk enough.

Fall
A few years older, the lawyers
know music, invite her to listen.
Leaves were burned in those days,
their incense drifting to the third floor,
where entranced novice hears Beethoven's Seventh,
as day slowly turns to dusk.

Winter
They stomp noisily through snowy streets,
the dark night crisp and promising.
Ancient, revered, the Brattle awaits, offering the sacred
Casablanca, their first viewing. Walking home,
they gaze in silence at the black sky.

Spring
She works at home one air-free May day.
Her knight appears, sweeps her care-free away,
his steed a Chevrolet. Spinning courtroom tales,
he drives to a wind-blown bay, upon whose strand
they splash, all sea-spray and sand.
She waves now, time and space in thrall,
to Mr. Lane, so happy to recall.

Summer
Her roommate calls from the stairwell.
Hurry, before the light dies!
They run like children to the bridge,
the Charles River alive with sunset.
Laughing, they fling their arms to the sky,
inhale the cool evening air, fading colors,
the glory of their youth,
this blessed time.

Lake Suite

In Summer

Forested hills rise black-green where
corners of New York and Vermont meet,
a blend of farms and villages,
their names reflecting landscape:
Glens Falls, Hoosick Falls—and history:
Salem, Cambridge, Greenwich.

Stony soil yet offers unequaled
apples, tomatoes, and sweet corn.
Glacial lake waters gleam,
cattle graze unperturbed.

Depression-and-city-bred, my parents
had modest means, horizons.
Whence came the imagination,
the will to build for their family
a cottage in this small Eden?

Reverie

Memory plays, as it will.
I wake to a sunlit
summer morning
at a cottage
in New England woods.

My mother is frying eggs
in bacon grease, as we did
in the nineteen-fifties.

A shoreline lane leads to the pump house.
Mornings, we take water to the well
for priming, thin sun-browned arms
forcing the day's ration into jugs,
heavy on the walk home.

We are perched on a hill
above the lake, a mile of
blue mirror one day, sheet
of ruffled charcoal the next.

Seen from our porch,
the lake's mood beckons.
This aerie's children
heed the call, water
giving life to our summer days.

On warm nights, we swim by moonlight,
noon-bright or veiled and pale.
Coming out cold, we shake ourselves
like the puppies we are,
hover over a small fire.

Airborne

for rm, in memoriam

Local fiddlers tune up, drums patter,
launch jaunty sounds into the summer night.
Taking the floor, your sorcerer's feet
never quite touch earth—whole body
shimmers, inches aloft.

Aglow from unseen sun, you embrace
the music, breathe the lakeside air,
while sparks of light prance on dark water
so close some nights dance leads to swim.

Gliding with liquid rhythm, languid
yet lively long limbs, you are king to
each partner's queen, floating as one
in a dream of dance.

To adolescent eyes, it is clear.
You were dropped, like Astaire from Olympus,
to elevate earthlings, show us buoyancy
on the wing.
You are sixteen.

After Sixty Years

Recent owners painted the cottage,
built a sturdy wooden staircase
down the hill where once through brush
and bramble we daily scrambled.

Memories flood the minds of visiting
octogenarians who step down stairs
to the timeless lakefront,
water now a flat gray,
quiet in midweek.

Steep hillside paths lead to the old barn,
promise of milk still foaming in a pail,
scent and sight, echoes of a distant day,
of rust-colored cow and new-mown hay.

II

MIDDAY

Scenes from a Marriage

No Exceptions

In the early seventies, jogging
became the new panacea,
secret to long, healthy life.
Reading the newspaper,
she noticed a news item:
Two physicians, vegetarians,
long-time runners
out for their morning jog. A heart
attack. One died.

At that time and place,
this was not
supposed to happen.

Astonished, she read the account
to her spouse. *How can this be? The man
did everything he could. And still . . .*

Her husband replied instantly,
*Dear one, do you truly imagine
the forces that govern the universe
are held in suspension
because a man jogs?*

Survival Tools

Their baggage stood by the door.
As she downed a hasty breakfast
before the taxi arrived,
he noted that a closet needed
earnest attention.

She waited three beats
and lied, *Did you know
reliable statistics prove
that women with four children
and demanding husbands
lose all hope, ALL hope
of EVER finishing ANYthing?*

He waited just one beat.
New England Journal of Medicine?

Half a beat. *National Geographic, May issue.*

Am I a demanding husband?

Just fancy numbers . . .

Not Funny, Just Ridiculous

After a late-night debate,
she clomped out of their room,
dragging pillow and blanket,
as a child pulls a beloved,
bedraggled bear.

Issues unresolved, all but forgotten,
had returned with startling force.

They both spoke English
on some occasions,
but she often lapsed into cuneiform,
he into quadratic equations . . .

Almost Awake

Afloat in the nightmind,
drifting in vapors of memory,
I think dawn thoughts
of all that is gone, what was done,
said—not done, not spoken.
Floating in a fog of regret.

Long awake, you appear,
the smell of burnt toast,
but you are smiling,
morning-ready.

Firstborn

for kem

Fresh young bud
turns and finds
the light she seeks;
in time, petals open.
Kathryn is our new light.

Children

Perfect Daughter

for Kathryn

I.
Nothing prepares—no book, no mentor,
no earnest friend. All describe, explain,
warn—to no avail.
The arrival of a firstborn—incommunicable,
orchestration unimagined.

II.
We did not raise you,
simply watched you grow—
eager to learn, try the new,
give widely of time and self.
Come, I'll show you how . . .

III.
Now grown, a mother (*your* title now).
Devotion floods your loyal soul,
finding joy in your son, daughter,
as they grow, so soon away.

IV.
Sufficient now to gaze at your own,
like their mother, still wondrous,
still perfect, every day.

The Artist

for Kevin

Born to make art, your myriad gifts
arrived early. At four, sparring,
using logic on your beleaguered mother.
Winning.

At seven, cartoons emerged,
your drawings brisk, minimal,
the satire preternatural.
Then parodies, comic sketches,
draped in accents droll, persuasive.
New talents by sixteen—
for math, science, cycling.
Music, no.

Capricious fate decreed a key change.
You biked the world, won your way,
but your true summit would be found,
not in a land of work or word,
but one of melody and chord.
The violin's haunting sound.

With your discipline, passion—
once for cycling high and wild—
then, transposed by love,
you became teacher, mentor, driver,
serving music and your beloved child.

The Shepherd

for Colin

Age three, your arms circle my legs
as you look up and ask,
Mom, are you having a bad day?
(Which, in fact, I am.)
My friend whispers, *An old soul.*

In Montana, our family of six
climbs a hill, the path narrow, stony.
Youngest stumbling, brave on this day.
You, not yet five, patrol, monitor all—
so many roots, boulders, sticks.
Someone might stray, lose the way.

We called you Shepherd then;
though your reach is now beyond our ken,
a shepherd you have ever been.

God's Gentle Warrior

for Chris

How could we have begun to imagine that you—
who emptied the entire contents of a medicine cabinet
on the carpet, who poured salt all over a dinner table
carefully set for twelve, who inspired with your devilry
your mild-mannered mother who had scoured the city
to find a tiny guitar for your musical three-year-old self,
only to stomp it flat late Christmas Day—that you
would become the man who writes sermons,
letters to make men weep and mothers rejoice;
who bathes dying men at Mother Teresa's
Sisters of Charity, who with such inner beauty seems
utterly unaware of your outer beguilement, all the while
not as devoted to tennis as to our God in heaven,
though now and then those in the stands might wonder.

So Many Boys

I realize, boys, that noise
defines your existence.
You pursue its many modes
with percussive persistence.
Cries of alarm, crashes,
and wreckage—
your life's subsistence.

Such consists for normal souls
of a fading resistance . . .

Come now, sturdy lads,
we need your assistance,
and pray daily
for your cease and desistance.

Things I Hate (not necessarily in that order)

ruminations by Kevin Moran, age 12,
Flint, Michigan, 1979

I hate the word yuppie.
I hate people who answer a question with a question.
I hate toasters that don't have a pop-up switch.
I hate people who think they get to read the whole news-
    paper at one time.
I hate people who spend all day shopping and don't buy
    anything.
I hate the grass that grows next to trees when you mow
    the lawn.
I hate fishing in the rain.
I hate eating lunch while people try to find the perfect
    size teabag right next to your table.
I hate pots that let the water leak through when you try
    to water the plants.
I hate cars that don't have any brake lights.
I hate people who put the cap on the toothpaste all the
    time.
I hate people who read the back side first.
I hate people who put on their turn signal four miles be-
    fore they turn.
I hate the sound a cockroach makes when you step on it.
I hate wet towels.
I hate the weeds at the bottom of the lake.

I hate people who use the word up when they don't have
    to.
I hate trying to sweep up the pine needles that get be-
    tween the cracks in the sidewalk.
I hate the word tasty.
I hate pictures that are off-center.
I hate places that charge money for the water.
I hate salad as the main course.
I hate game shows.
I hate waitresses that keep asking you how you are doing.
I hate waitresses that say they'll be right back.

I hate people who hate things for no good reason.

Story Matters

Stories spoken and sung,
rising from page or tongue.
Brother, sister,
breadcrumb trails.
Saintly lions, enticing mice,
baffled bears.
Wise pig prevails
to sup on wolf stew.
Repentant rabbit
sips chamomile brew.
Foes, fiery dragons come,
honor lost, then won.

Awakened in such ways,
we grow to love old tales
and tell them all our days.

College President's Wifery

We Do The Best We Can

In those days, the tea was for wives
of faculty members—teaching done most
often by men. Her husband a research
assistant, she barely qualified.

Insecure, but curious, she attended.
Mrs. President's Wife, in royal blue,
each strand of silver hair
in its own placid place,
greeted each guest with a gaze
resting at the hairline.
Welcome to the President's Home.

Three years passed; another college,
another tea, an older Mrs. PW who,
with unpolished nails and no noticeable
interest in fashion, greeted newcomers,
engaged each woman eagerly.

Wasn't the fall glorious this year?
Can you manage our Boston winters?
We're not New York, but we have our Symphony.
Or do you prefer jazz?
When all else failed,
What does your family do on weekends?

A decade after the tea of silver hair,
yet another college, another tea.
A shift now, stunning reversal.
Newly-resident in the President's Home,
baby and toddler asleep upstairs;
with her husband, she greeted the men
and women of the faculty,
aware that every hair was not in place,
the floor—where late the ping-pong table lived—
was scuffed, and that her sons,
arriving soon from school,
would rebuff her stare,
silently scavenge for scones.

Ah, Mr. Jones, are your Biology students lively?
Turning to his wife, *Dr. Jones, does your Physics
lab equal your husband's over in Biology?*
(Oh dear, perhaps not a good question . . .)
And finally, safely,
What does your family do on weekends?

SarahSally, Alan—1974

for sjv

You radiate tenderness and
fierce energy, deploying that rare
blend to serve a desperate world.
You turn to your flute; filigreed silver
sound invites listeners—who travel on clouds—
to your own place of serene and
inexpressible grace.

In his later years, the great South African,
Alan Paton, came to campus for the spring;
readers thronged, carrying cherished copies
of *Cry, The Beloved Country.* Our factory city
embraced Mr. Paton—dinners, picnics,
garden-gatherings. *Please call me Alan . . .*

Having seen deeply into your saint's heart,
—a reflection of his own—he would seek
you, find two chairs, his dear curmudgeon's eyes
alight at the sight and sounds of Sally.

I, too, saw your heart,
my guide before I knew
it was time to learn.

Much Ado About Nuttin'

She managed the first decade
as wife of a college president
without owning
a silver nut spoon.
During year eleven,
she was notified, harshly,
that her domicile was devoid
of this sterling shell-shape.

Why do some people own
nut spoons, while others do not?
Ah, therein lie many tales,
of culture, history, domesticity,
and whether Aunt Tilda's legacy
of silver included
a nut spoon.

Perhaps, lacking an Aunt Tilda,
We may recall woe and yearning,
glimmers of hope, a bit of learning.
She gathered, over several decades
of wifery, many tales to tell—
none featuring a nut spoon,
until now. Just as well.

With gratitude to poet Connie Ralston for the inspired title.

An Inauspicious Introduction

for wfb and ptb, in memoriam

More than a few privileges enriched
her unpaid work, such as the first weekend
at the harbor-side home in Connecticut.

Her host, the man who famously stood
athwart history yelling stop, the man
said to prefer being governed by the first
hundred names in the Boston Telephone Book
than the faculty of Harvard,
laboriously carried her suitcase
from the car to the guest room.

It's on rollers, she offered feebly, unwilling
to question the judgement
of so worldly a man.

This most generous and courtly of men grumbled,
Damned if I know why people bring so much
for a simple weekend in the country.
Mortified, but still vertical, she murmured,
Insecurity breeds a need for more clothing.

He harrumphed again, then softened,
a kind man after all, perhaps abashed by her discomfort,
perhaps mindful of the woman in residence,
spouse of fifty years, six feet of model-thin
fashion-forward *femme fatale,*
who appeared for cocktails swathed in scarlet
chiffon wearing a red hat three-feet wide,
having prepared alone the meal we would soon
joyfully inhale, and whose own luggage was
by no means light.

Eudora Welty's Saving Grace

Eudora Welty came to dinner
one spring evening. Her host,
anticipating lively, even brilliant talk,
assembled all manner of lit'ry folk.
Writers, professors of English,
a Welty scholar, filled the table,
Ms. Welty at its head,
hopeful, hapless hostess at its foot.

As salad plates were removed,
the meal's fate was already sealed.
Conversation was to be—limited.
With mounting dismay, poor host
watched sheer silence unfold.
Each guest, revered by students,
dared not state the obvious, nor ask
an imperfect question, before peers.
No, he must watch and wait.

Laughter, jolly chatter from nearby tables
crushed the chosen, miserable few.
At last, the divine Eudora, in her eighties,
on a demure white horse at full gallop,
reined in at the table and reigned,
thereby saving the huddled mass
from further excruciation.

She spoke, her voice a rivulet
rippling over pebbles and mossy mounds,
then a trilling mockingbird, who well
understood the comedy unspooled below.
She spoke of her life, told stories,
offered earnest inquiries.

Eudora Welty's pure heart warmed worried souls,
allowed even wilted host to breathe again.
All questions, every comment, they now knew,
would be perfect.

Dessert was chocolate, and the first raspberries of spring.

In addition to her body of work, Eudora Welty was known for the lilting Mississippi rhythms of her speaking voice, as well as her immense kindness to all she encountered.

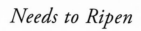

Needs to Ripen

Hearing You

If I am to listen, truly hear you,
I must hurl myself into your trench.
I've heard it before,
often gather wool
as you speak.

You offer a child's laments,
a parent's regrets, friend's ailment,
worker's fatigue.

But if I am to serve you well,
my friends, my loved ones,
I must come to attention,
leave the wool for another day.

If I am to listen, truly hear you,
I must hurl myself into your trench.

You Would?

If you saw
what I saw,
if you heard
what I heard,
and knew
what I know,
would you do
what I must do?

Bushwhacking

How do you manage?
Solving problems—too many
shapes and sizes—some cosmic,
theologic, existentic.

Time—never enough. Suddenly,
too much. Family—too much.
Later—not enough.

Work—worries and wonders,
technical, personal, mythical.

Maintenance—leaking pipes, fraying cords
on lamps or loved ones. Short circuits
of all kinds.

So, do you choose wit, your native genius?
Do you cogitate, meditate, agitate?
Procrastinate, prevaricate, and if all else fails,
placate?

Or do you research? Find experts
on sick puppies, trick elbows,
matters of the heart—
so much coming apart.

Perhaps you pursue wise friends,
counselors? Pray for guidance?

Or do you plunge in, feet first,
forge ahead, churning,
burning with purpose
if not clear vision.

Yes, all of the above. But it's all
bushwhacking, friends. Just
bushwhacking.

Transcript

for ld and wem

Some decades ago,
a dry Northern wind blew down,
chose to remain in the Southern clime.
Natives shivered, sought defenses.

In time, cool air warmed slightly,
sting softened, melted
into old-time ways.
Responding, locals shed armor,
cares, fretted less.

Steadily, imperceptibly, each leaned
towards its opposite, growing gently
into what it was always
meant to be.

With Deep Regret

Ours was one of the Faculty Wives clubs
that flourished on campuses for decades—
Book groups, cooking clubs, French speakers,
hikers, even a few bikers. We were music.
Recorders. Very serious.

Dainty birch sopranos, sturdy altos,
handsome shining tenors for longer fingers.
We played joyfully and with diligence.
Vivaldi, Palestrina, a bit of Bach.
Then coffee, gossip, and laughter.

After several years, a newcomer
to our Eden—
much younger, big hair, small skirt.
Girlish cheer to our exurban
New Yorkishness.
Shirlene played the accordian.

After all, the club newsletter listed
Music Group, not *Baroque Music Only*.
She played popular songs—
at family parties, weddings.
Shirlene had never seen a recorder.

Eight well-meaning musicians were courteous,
but unable to confront ancient questions:
the group, the individual; Art and its imperatives.
Courtesy, kindness . . . alas.

Dear Reader, what would you have done?

Belt . . . and Suspenders

The poet spoke of peaches
and trousers rolled.
A near-century later,
what of the cautious soul?

The need to choose
plagues the favored few—
much yet to brew.

Observe, reflect, decide, act.
Could, should, must, ought.
The balance daily sought.
How long for Observe?
How long Reflect?

When does caution turn
to lasting indecision, options
open, ever open?

Will you be girded always
by doubt? Suspended forever,
neither in, nor out.

Taste for Mink

My friend is an old soul,
kind and wise beyond her years.
Wants a simple life, pared down,
likes to give things away.

One blustery winter day,
she revealed the coat, an aunt's gift,
fresh from storage.
I wasn't made for this, she murmured,
draping it over my shoulders.

Thinking, *Nor was I,*
I slid into the satin lining,
ever ready to sacrifice
for a friend.

Cocooned to my toes in a cloud
of honey-hued light and air, I felt no weight,
only warmth. Playing dress-up, I danced,
pranced before a dark mirror.

Unrealistic of course—the beloved aunt,
her heartfelt gift. We parted in high spirits,
happy in our long friendship.

But in the inmost folds of my woolen coat, something small, dangerous, and delicious stirred to life.

Pas de Deux

The call came from the deep past.
Thirty years since they'd been freshman
in that august, remote, and forested place.
The name was unfamiliar.
He persisted, *I left in January,*
never returned. Saw you often
that first fall. You said my socks
didn't match my shirt.
She remembered nothing.
Well, I'll be in town all week,
if you want to have lunch.

Peeling potatoes for six, baking chicken,
brushing teeth, she searched her memory,
to no avail.
Did matching socks and shirts *ever* matter?
Had she been so rude and callous?

In a pre-dawn hour, his face swam up
from some ancient, unimagined corridor.
The sweet, eager boy
from a small hill town. Pale skin,
a resistant spike of brown hair.
Earnest talks, woodland walks.
A single kiss, chaste and shy.

Only in hindsight could she see—
the gray crewneck had been
his single and dear-bought claim
to Ivy style. Anxious herself,
she had missed his ache
in that status-ridden sea.

Then, on top of the socks,
she had erased him . . .
A telephone call, apologies,
plans for lunch.

He looked his age, but only just.
She, unaccustomed to being surveyed
so thoroughly, hastened into the motel
restaurant booth, excusing to herself
his choice of venue—her city, not his.

He spoke of success in business,
lively wife, grown sons, golf, a pool.
Pleasant enough, he seemed detached, afloat.
Were motel cafes indeed his terrain?

He had written, illustrated his first book.
Friends found it funny. *I'll send you a copy.*
If you're not a prude.
Oh, but I am, she said unsmiling.
Undeterred, he went on,
It's about men and their various ways.

Conversation turned more purposeful.
His eyes glittered as he nodded
toward the elevator, thus clarifying
his selection of a meeting place.
He knew his turf.
Are you suggesting . . . ?

For the socks.

Annoyance held laughter in check;
girl in gingham, she had walked in.
Here I am with Willy Loman, ludicrous
attention to be paid . . .

Carefully, diligently, she bantered,
asked questions, ran out the clock.
This would have to do,
and it did. They split the bill,
their leave-taking polite, final.

The book arrived, a prurient pamphlet
on male body parts, their tendency
toward waywardness and misadventure,
jauntily illustrated.
Disinclined to offer such unsavory stew
to her sons, she cremated the compendium,
and placed in a bin of melancholy
the tainted memories
of a fresh-faced boy,
his cowlick.

Willy Loman is the protagonist in Arthur Miller's great play
Death of a Salesman.

Falling Backward

Plastic bags floating
in the duck pond.
Climbing down,
saving ducks from danger,
her foot slipped.

An obscure law of physics
flung her into space—
back swan dive
into eighteen inches
of sullen water.

She emerged from submersion,
plastic prize her work,
sunhat and dignity
lost in murk.

Years later, she concluded
that falling backward
was a clear sign
of much to come.

III

BEYOND THE BURROW

As The Stricken World Grows More So

As it spins and plummets,
what defenses can we muster?
We, grandfather, grandmother
in our eighth decades, still parents daily,
relatively sound of mind and body,
but no longer as eager or able
to save the world.

You have your books, German Shepherd,
rain-or-shine dawn walks.
I, not given to morning mobility,
have the dark bitter brew that,
while lacking the kick of caffeine,
still offers it own modest consolation
as I turn fresh brittle pages,
inhaling news of life
beyond our burrow.

Filling Spaces

September 11, 2001

What fills a space,
a place, a land
until its heart bursts
and comes apart?

Ashes float, drift, scatter
land, never fill,
are still
deadly matter.

Smoke fills a space,
a place, a land,
chokes, steals air, defiles
a child's face.

Fire fills, consumes a space,
a land, leaves smoke and ash
to hide the parched,
now buried place.

Hate fills a space, a land
when the hating heart bursts,
devours, burns all to sand.

Unspeakable sounds fill the dead gray air, until in time a
new sound rises from the howling fire, from the dying
land of ash and smoke.

The tender songs of souls, their falling tears streaming
down, down, a freshet to cool the searing pain, rain of
tears bathing the lost beloved; tear-salted waters rush to
declare a fresh new river, a new river to soothe a land
riven no more.

so we did fervently hope . . .

*This poem was featured in a New York gallery show in 2001.
Several stanzas were later engraved on a commemorative steel
sculpture by artist Jim Gallucci.*

April Fury

Early spring, a quiet city.
Dogwoods bloom, innocent
pink and white against a darkening sky.

Afternoon air turns heavy,
blue-black clouds crack open,
hurl slashing rain. Screaming winds
wield a sky-big scythe
across a thousand-foot swath,
sixteen miles of tidy homes and shops,
bright azaleas, green lawns.

Sheared-off trees take wing,
like mammoth vultures—
agents of havoc smash,
puncture rooftops, choke streets,
split homes like logs.

Caprice reigns with such rains.
Did Nature have a list?
Strike this, pass over that.
A schoolhouse roof caves in
as playground swings stand intact,
inches from an oak that topples,
leaves a crater yards-wide,
rootball reaching the sky.

Untouched,
two birdhouses on slender poles
are prim soldiers guarding ruins
just yards away.

People trapped in homes, others
flee as walls crash in, ceilings explode.
Where will I sleep tonight?
And tomorrow?

The city rallies. Rescuers, repairmen,
volunteers by the hundreds.
Food, clothing, bedding, dollars pour in.
Officials arrive, do what officials do.
Rebuilding begins—shattered homes,
battered lives.

Howling banshees won the first round.
Patience, courage, heart win the next.
Greensboro prevails.

Here and There

Belatedly, the suburban mother
notes the snug fit
of her young child's shoes.
Massaging the little foot,
You didn't complain, she says.
No, but I was crying in my head.

In the harsh light of war-torn Sudan
a mother clutches her child
as horsemen pillage and destroy.
Her village is dead.
She will cry forever
in her head.

This poem was written soon after I worked with Anthony Anei Majok, a Lost Boy of Sudan, as he wrote his harrowing memoir Journey of Faith. The second stanza here might well be about Anthony's mother.

Sed Libera Nos a Malo

A brief news item, few details.
Suffocation, mutilation, more.

Bestial, the police said.

*You could hardly tell
he was human,* the mother
had screamed, meaning
his remains, her son,
her child.

It seems a rougher beast
than poets conjure
has slouched to foul birth
in this deadly time.

*Sed libera nos a malo is from the Lord's Prayer in Latin: Deliver
us from evil.*

Dies Irae (Politics 2020)

Despite our long friendship.
must my views
stir in you such rage
that you promise
to hurl glass
at the cold stone
of my grave?

Dies Irae is Latin for day of wrath.

IV

ALL FALL DOWN

Mostly Holes

She's there as I pick up mail.
Life is mostly holes, ain't it?
This was while we talked awhile
over the mop in the hall.

Um, I'm not sure what you mean?

Honey, I raised up six kids,
I loved 'em, but was I green.

But that's just grand. Isn't it?

Would be, could I find 'em all.
See my baby, she's one hole.
In my heart, that's where it is.
Can't find her no place, nowheres.

Did what I could, church and chore.
But that wrong crowd at the door,
they'll do. That hole yank her through.
Now never you mind my tears.

She been gone all these long years.

Not the Magi, 1930

Times were hard the Christmas
a young father, trying to bring glamour
into the life of his hard-pressed wife,
bought her a silk gown the color of dawn.

Opening it, with children gathered round,
she decried the extravagance, wept
in frustration—such waste of scarce dollars.

One year later, the children watched, tense,
then relieved, as their mother unwrapped
her gift: a bulb for the living room lamp,
whose light of late had gone dim.

Conjuring Carmen, Conjuring Eve

She is temptress, vixen.
Possessed, moth to her flame,
Don Jose kills Carmen.
Victim becomes villain.
Who is to blame?

Has he not fallen first, lured
from home, love, livelihood?
Taken by fever dream.

Strange, such tales,
retold for centuries,
written by men
to blend and blur
villain and victim.

Eve too, cast as temptress, not
the progenitor nature decreed,
Adam her Don Jose.

Was it always thus agreed?
To confuse those who read
and wonder, about
victim and villain.
So simple to mislead.

Mean Streak

It lies hidden,
waits to rise
unbidden
into the light
bringing darkness.

Why wound
those we love?
Why not cherish
and protect?

Oh we do, we do.
Kindness is basic,
a habit of faith
to practice
and renew.

And yet, and yet.
As the infecting shaft
breaks through
it pierces me,
and you.

Green Shoot

When she wounded him,
his heart burst,
sending pieces skyward.
They fell in time on distant lands.

Years passed. Seized by remorse,
she scoured the earth,
searched out every piece,
sewed them together.

Seeking him out, she offered his heart
on a bed of wild thyme—petals
of penance—and dandelion,
teeth of the lion.
Too late.
His eyes filled as he refused
his heart, turned away.

She planted the heart, facing north,
watered it daily, pallid root.
Might she in time see a green shoot
gain strength,
spring lively forth?

Fable: Dialogue on Marrying Up

A long, long while I searched for you,
said the Shepherd. *Found you at last,*
widowed, closed in a golden castle.
I have only silver and my flock.

I waited for you to find me,
she replied. *Now you must*
scale the tower. Mind the shadows—
of prince and princeling—tall one gone,
small one beside me.

Your castle is miles and mountains
from my grazing lands. Gold, shadows
surround and protect you.
What can I provide?

Your constancy exceeds my treasure.

An eavesdropping scholar interrupted,
In older tales than this, the shepherd
must stalk the dragon, enter the dark
wood, and cross the swamp alone.
Prize and princess wait at rainbow's end.

The shepherd who was neither old nor young,
replied, *Those tales were left unfinished.*
After the search, the brave deeds, the winning,
comes the life. Will the shepherd's flock
find welcome in the bower? Will they miss
their fields? Must the man live without his sheep?
He is a shepherd after all.

Those issues, said the scholar, *were not*
covered in the old tales.

Accumulation

The book should be enshrined
on the mantel, a cautionary tale
for his acquisitive family.

The story for children
describes a race of messy folk,
the Pollutians. After filling
every corner of their world,
they pared down
to a thousand possessions each,
then decamped,
started over on an empty planet.

Too much, he thought.
So many wives, so few children.
Too much house, stuffed, clotted
with what? Nothing.
Nothing we couldn't leave,
find a new life—
somewhere.

How does the children's story end?
Oh, cheerfully!
Three or four planets later,
the Pollutians persist, ever onward.

The book itself?
Pushed from the mantel,
lost in the dust,
the household debris.

Unfortunately, The Pollutians is no longer in print. Perhaps it was taking up too much space?

Sometimes an Equation

Dorianne was thrifty with praise,
lavish in her critiques.
Doled out compliments
once a year or so.
Or was it once a decade?

He said it was once a marriage.

*Do you think sometimes
you might . . . ?* he would ask.

This is the way I am,
she would inject.

As they grew older, he felt fine.
She did not.

So this is what happens,
she lamented.

This is the way you are,
Mr. Gray whispered,
one hand resting lightly
on her chair as
oiled wheels
turned slowly.

Small Mercies

Two young brothers bait hooks
at a fishing pier on the Maine coast.
Click! A reporter takes their picture
for the morning edition—neglecting
to ask their permission.

The paper later sells the photo. *Baiting Boys*
appears on billboards, magazines,
fishing tackle labels. Ernie and Tim
cut out their image, press in a book.

Years pass. When Ernie dies, Tim seeks a memento.
The old clipping so faded, slightly torn—
a real print could be framed,
set up on the mantel.

After much travail, Tim—a resolute Maine man,
after all—finds an archive.

He must buy his own image. The clerk notes
Tim's humble demeanor, gives him a discount.

On second thought, she slips in extra prints.

V

NOT JUST ABOUT THE FOOD

Easter Tea at the Ritz

feastification: to be edified and educated
while eating too much

A sublime celebration
decorative, architectural, and culinary,
strands of a tapestry
designed to enchant.

The setting—gilded-era opulence.
Fretwork ceiling sends a sunrise glow,
walls, carpets gleam with roseate warmth.
Faint traces of British restraint—and noble
cascades of fresh lilies, chrysanthemums, tulips.

Pristine pink table linen. Delicate
rosebud china, shining silver.
Piano music—Gershwin, Kern, Mercer.
Champagne-surprised teen grandchildren,
who sip with cautious delight.
Waiters wear tuxedos with red vests,
a hint perhaps—no haughtiness here.

Is it the two adolescents, absorbing every detail, eagerly
consuming sweet and savory, scone and cake,
who bring a twinkle to the eye of each waiter,
pleased with his power to offer delicacies
to these perceptive innocents?

Easter Tea at the Ritz, The Menu

First, the tea, a pot each, chosen from a menu of many.
The savories—trays of finger sandwiches—
ham and mustard-butter, cucumber and fresh dill,
chicken with sage sauce, egg and chive.

The sweets: intense lemon macarons, pomegranate
mocha tarts, floating meringues, apricot-almond bars.

Eloise, defending her rivalrous Plaza,
might have said, *That was* hardly *enough!*

Scones arrive warm, each with silver bowls
of raspberry jam, clotted cream.
The finale, as if needed—ginger chocolate torte.

We need do this just once in a lifetime.
Perhaps twice . . .

With several senses serenely sated, our party of five
thanks the endearing gentlemen who fed and feted us,
then stumble out of our rosy-gold fantasy
into raging London rain—soon to be a named hurricane.

Easter Tea at the Ritz, The Dream

Your sleep, fitful that night,
served with a slice of guilt—
the sour price of excess.

Mist drifts across the mind—
now, yours is a different family in transit.

Your village burned by hordes in black hoods,
you fled, endured a ragged sea-crossing.
Then miles on foot, your son
carrying one child, his wife the other.

You eat scraps, barely-ripened
berries, water by the drop.
A month before, neighbors came for tea,
lilies in a glass, figs from your tree.

At last the border. A gray-brown landscape,
flimsy tents, huddled masses.
You find a place to stand, plywood
gradually sinking in the mud.

Your family is with you, alive.
Today is Easter Sunday.

Sunday Brunch

Before New York cafes became bistros,
the tiny West Side "EATS"
stepped out from film noir, just for them,
a mother and daughter fresh up from the polite South.

Jarring style of service—she slapped menus
on faux-marble. *Okay girls, what'll it be?*

At least a hundred and ten years old, bent over,
still shuffling around a place like this, clearly
not the owner. How then could they mind
when without words she slammed down
plates of dark bacon, dubious eggs, burnished toast,
coffee sloshing over cups, no saucer in sight.

The hands that served breakfast were gnarled,
but tipped by delicate oval nails, manicured to perfection,
American Beauty Rose. Silvery blond hair, waved and
elegant. A wig? It didn't matter.

She brought the modest bill. The daughter said,
*Excuse me, Ma' m, but your hands, your hair are
so beautiful; we've been admiring you.*

Thanks honey, the waitress said, unsmiling.
*Without this hair, these nails,
I'd kill myself.*

How to Eat Chocolate

It is not mere confection, as initiates know.
True chocolaphiles love deep chocolate,
sixty percent cacao, a dark, murky velvet.
Luscious, bittersweet, holy mud.

Should the convert choose
to probe mythic depths and heights,
sample wine-like symphonic notes
and overtones—and this is only
about chocolate, remember—
then, my friends, sugar must go.
Sweetness deceives tender taste buds,
offending their delicate dignity.
Seduced by vile white crystals,
the novice *chews* the cold chunk,
finds only cloying, puny flavor.
The precious moment squandered.

Poor postulant knows not
the slow warming melt
in the mouth's moist oven
of sixty percent cacao,
the divine swirl, the gentle yielding essence,
a final dark elixir emerging,
sliding down at last
into sublime
memory.

Radishes with Relish

Slicing into plump radishes
took her back full circle.

Back to a summer day—
two students making potato salad.
One insists on a market visit,
just for radishes, explaining,
Mother was firm—proper potato salad
needs radishes. For color and crunch.

Eager novice soon agreed—
a lesson in culinary detail.
Years passed.

For her hungry family of six
she prepared and served
approximately forty seven-thousand
meals, mostly without radishes,
an odd vegetable after all.

She made the first twenty-nine
thousand with relish. At about thirty
thousand, slowing down, but family fond
of food, she slogged on to forty-seven
thousand with lemon zest, yes,
but with much less relish,
her brain having turned to oatmeal.
By then, fewer people graced the table;
meals became ever-simpler.
Summer of the forty-seven thousandth
meal—having long since abandoned recipes,
she inexplicably opened a dusty cooking tome,
soon mixed garbanzos with caraway, tried
the humble parsnip, carrots in cream.

Farm stand vegetables were fine that year.
Slicing long-forgotten radishes, so fat and rosy,
she noted the sharp knife and firm board, easy cutting
rhythm, the view from her window sunny,
all yellow-green.

As forty-seven thousand approached, she smiled—
surprised to relish simple glory after
an infinity in food.

Sacramental Pickles

for Fred and Susan, Mark and Beth,
and Bill, who blessed the meal

With much tenderness
the host placed his jar
of cornichons
at table center.

Sacred act, or mere merriment?
Yes.

A guest offered praise for picking
these particular pickles.

Observed another, *Please note*
the putting of pickles so perfectly
in their place.

And everyone laughed and fell to.

124

Tyranny of Dinner

As late afternoons
pile high year in, year out,
like mounds of fallen leaves,
she is anchored, always,
by meal and menu.

Who but the daily practitioner
of this science, this art, can know
the tyranny of Dinner?

If the sacred Meal is to progress
with a modicum of success,
she must take heed:
plans, purchases must precede
the slice and chop,
the simmer, saute, stir, flip,
and occasional flop.

Quick, the serving while food is hot.
Panting chef corrals folk
from up, down, in, out.

Dinner at last. A merciful veil
here descends on random
cross-fire, not quite
conversation.

Day's center, yet weary finale,
dinner is more and less than
it should be, could be . . .

On the Other Hand

for Ryder and his Dad

She navigates the crowded market aisles,
pondering the arrival of eldest son and child.
They could dine out—too hard
for a toddler. At Grandpa's house
books, trucks, blocks with Dad.

Ah, Dover sole, moist and fresh.
Just in this morning! beams the counterman.
They discuss the vagaries of weather,
as he wraps two pounds of gleaming fillets.
She finds tender young asparagus, notices
plump lemons. *Two, please.*

Since she married one Irishman, then birthed
a batch, potatoes are next,
such luxury to buy prepared. Finally,
smooth white mushrooms and fluffy lettuce.
Laden with provisions, a spring in her step,
home to saute mushrooms
and roast asparagus.

Starving Artist

Her commute was longer,
so he made the family dinner.
Planning ahead, he'd extract
time from late evening
like juice from a cold lemon.

One night he peeled apples,
the next, made crust,
the third, baked his creation.

Tastes good, his wife said,
but mother served it with cheddar.
No ice cream? his son complained.
Hmmm, thought the man,
did not make pie again.

One night he peeled, cubed, and salted eggplant,
the next, roasted tomatoes, onions, peppers,
the third, baked his creation.

Tastes good, his wife said, *but no garlic?*
No meat? his son complained.

The next day the man bought food-like items,
microwaved a green thing.
Tastes good! said his wife.
Tastes good! said his son.
Thus did their food devolve.
Dessert now arrives in cellophane.

Old Age Young

As the curtain came down
I felt a tap. *It's fifty years
since I've been in this theater.
Can you tell me what's changed?*
Her hair was brown and waved, eyes bright,
though the body suggested her many years.
Wheelchair on the aisle. *My Cadillac!*
as she slapped the seat.

I'm revising my cookbook, she confided.
*Single room, no kitchen. But my computer converts
the recipes, helps me update them
for younger tastes*—arugula, cilantro, harisse, kale.
And after that movie, pinot noir! Her computer?
So rare then, emails on the far horizon.

Suggestions for sugarless pie offered
between acts two and three. *You'll love it!*
Then sweet-and-sour chicken.
Best you'll ever taste. As final applause faded,
a recipe: blueberry relish. *Delicious!*

As a friend pushed the chair
into the night, she waved, calling out,
I'll send you a list of best cook books . . .

When She's Gone, None Can Say She Never Made Soup

Lesson learned early:
pour chicken broth from can, cube,
or actual chicken, into your best
cauldron. Choose three or four from
potato, tomato, turnip, onion,
spinach, squash, pumpkin, peas,
broccoli, carrots, celery.
Simmer awhile, cool, and send all
on a mad blender-spin with salt,
pepper, and za'atar. Soup!

Soup for lunch, for dinner,
and in-between, Soup forever . . .
When one makes Soup,
offers it every day—
trial, error along the way—
lessons learned will have
both much and little to do
with Soup.

If you find no wit in this verse,
consider life sans soup—
so much worse.

Tea With Rain

That particular window seat remains
my place for taking tea, watching rain.

Pewter-lined clouds—stages
for reverie, obscure, astray.
Skies not sunbright blue, just gray,
but glinting silver in the mind.
Rain, drizzle, the chill
of much slipping away.

Gleaming pungent pavement,
lamplight's amber glow indistinct—
blurred by drops that slip
down my windowpane. The hush
that blankets harsh street sounds.
The shy fragrance of moistened earth.

Only the tang of woodsmoke
haunts memory more
than the muffled music
of a drenching downpour.

Stan's Mother and Arnold

As Stan told it, a sow had turned on her litter
as non-human parents sometimes do
when they fail to bond with what God hath wrought.
One quart-sized piglet escaped.

My father warned Mother:
An orphaned piglet needs to be put down.
Raised a town girl, she put it down all right,
in a comfy box in her warm kitchen.

Good advice is mere words unless lived.
You never ever name livestock.
But Mother named and bottle-fed Arnold—
to corn-cracking size. Then moved him
to an old milking parlor to grow-off.
One frosty fall day, when bull calves became steers
and the last crops were put by,
Arnold relocated to the freezer.

Weeks later, guests eating pork unawares
would ask what was wrong with Mother
as she choked on mouthfuls amidst streaming tears
she would not wipe away.

*Stan Jenkins grew up in rural North Carolina in the 1950s
and '60s, then lived for years in Alaska. These words are taken,
virtually verbatim and with his permission, from a letter Stan
wrote to me about his beloved parents.*

Bitter Lemon

Nearly divine, the floating fragrance
of lemon blossom
reaches for glory.

Lemon makes the sweet piquant,
with honey soothes an angry throat,
with salt cleans all.
Irreplaceable, the healthy lemon,
ripe, tart, firm-skinned,
can abruptly turn soft, bitter—
odor acrid, flesh gray.

Why such rapid decay?
Mishap? Perhaps. Or loss
of will that once withdrawn
spawns collapse
within a day.

Watermelon

So hard to watch, listen.
Syria, for crying
out loud.
North Korea. Sudan.
The mind wants to close,
find distraction.

So pleasant then in summer
to take tomatoes from the vine,
slice cucumbers, peppers,
watermelon.

Miserere Nobis

Calamities occur daily. From raging
fires to ravaged lands, they come to us
over dinner.

Watching wars unfold in real time
on the home screen, we turn away
stunned. Or just stare, stop
breathing.

But soon enough, we lift forks
and chew.

From the Latin: Have mercy on us.

Santa Touria

for Touria Rimawi

Seven people, three generations of a family,
spend a week at Roman churches, basilicas
in the company of angels and saints.

Home, bedraggled and hungry,
here is their own angel, Touria,
saint of the culinary arts,
whose table rivals the finest osteria.

Fresh cod baked with tomato, panko, harisse,
and cilantro. Tender kale, tamed
by Touria. A mystical mix of herbs atop
thick eggplant rounds, ratatouille hiding magic
—sumac, ginger root, lemon, garlic, and za'atar.

I shop for freshest fish, says Touria, her accent Moroccan.
Outdoor markets for greens—so crisp!

A grandchild asks, *Miss Touria, did you
learn to cook growing up in Marrakesh?*

*Yes, I start there. But everywhere, I love the people.
They teach me.*

As the table is cleared, new aromas drift in
from Touria's temple. Cake arrives, delicate
custard topping a light crust, impossible
to imagine its creation.
Finally, lemon verbena tea, leaves
from the windowsill garden.

The family decides they will never travel again,
simply kneel forever at the shrine
of Santa Touria.

Dear-Bought Caras

In his eighth decade, a man often
spoiled at mealtime, inexplicably
turns to making fresh orange juice
for his aged wife.

He has discovered the Cara,
two of which produce sweetness
beyond describing,
an Olympic elixir.

Each morning he provides the golden cup.
Day after day, she rejoices, applying
a supply of superlatives acquired
over a lifetime.

The magic nectar is a spring tide. Yet,
in time, she notes an ancient dispute.
His swift reply, *Cara!* Reminder, baited
with blarney, Italian-style.

Something new/old has appeared
in their morning Eden. If not a snake,
at least an eel.

She hastens to pave over the complaint
and sighs, realizing she has been bought
again.

Ritual Revived

She grows impatient waiting
for gallons of water to boil
in the massive vessel. Finally,
the roiling ocean on the stove
receives a steel rack of jars packed
with marmalade—zesty orange,
piquant cranberry.

Twelve minutes in water boiling
over metal lids. Five minutes of rest,
and she lifts each glass *carefully*—
straight up through scalding bath.
Twenty-four hours to cool, labels affixed,
and the *'lades* are now gifts—holiday,
birthday, breakfast . . .

Sweet memories led to this labor—
her parents on hot August nights, peeling,
slicing crops green, yellow, red, filling
Mason jars, hovering over the steaming kettle,
preserving peaches, beans, tomatoes
from their small Victory garden,
enough to feed their children
for yet another wartime winter.

VI

NOT DIGNIFIED

I Wanna be an Intellectual

There was a time
when men of letters,
and women, two or three,
led liter'ry lives
unfettered and free.
Lived by wit and word
and were heard.
To my adolescent mind
that was neat.

Trouble was,
never read much,
especially books.
All those pages,
so many words.
I'd rather eat.

Little interest
in ideas, large
or small.
I was beat.

After many years, a friend,
misinformed, made a request:
You read a lot, she said.
Could you gather all you know
and make it into a short video?

And so I did, a mighty feat.
Now we can all be
the intellectual elite.

Fourth of July

Summer reminds us
we are a mammiverous land.
On Forty-Second Street or Main,
sun-lit sand, mountain path, coastal strand—
silicone-born or nature's own,
mammaries parade.

Quivering, bouncing, or eerily
still, they lead.

Brown, white, freckled
flags of flesh
wave in triumph to crowds agape.

Night falls.
Contained, barely, in bits
of knit, they compete.
Cascades of multivalent curvature
render fireworks obsolete.
The bright bulbous display bursts forth
             below eye level.

Time Plays

for lm

Her children were in school with mine
thirty years ago. We often confided—
the joys, heartaches of parenthood—
had not seen each other since.

I spotted her recently in a crowd.
Our eyes locked in mutual recognition:
huge smiles, outstretched arms, heartfelt embrace.
I used to love you, she cried out, *but now
I can't remember your name.*

Theorist

He strode to the lectern, black cape aswirl,
began to speak, mustaches atwirl.

Was his theory esoteric, or just enigmatic?
She found it deeply problematic—
pragmatic, or slyly emblematic?

She concluded he was, in fact,
merely epigrammatic,
belonging to the ages at last,
in grandpa's attic.

Oops! Deflection, 1960

A celebrated gentleman,
twice her age and more.
Collided in the dining car,
Century Limited.

At dinner, fine conversations. Thus,
grand by his own and others' estimations,
he arrived at her compartment
with high expectations.

How avuncular you are! said she,
Might you find an elder to please?
And I? As it happens,
I am grievously afflicted
with hoof and mouth disease.

City Boy After Too Much Wordsworth

Nature is nice.
I watched it twice.
Birds flew over,
grass grew under.

Dip in the sea.
Wet, cold as ice.
Nature is nice,
but not for me.

This tale was inspired in part by a transplant from New York City to beautiful Michigan. He missed his Broadway shows, the Metropolitan Opera. Being helpful, I said, But look at what's here, the lakes, the forests . . .

I hate trees, he said, and walked away.

Language Lite

Bark on beech
mottled and gray
announces pattern
its own quiet way.

Bark on beach,
dripping and gruff
announces loudly
water enough!

Barque on beach,
along the Nile.
To scholars who smile:
I've waited awhile.

Wanda and Gertrude

Over eighty, widowed for decades,
Wanda found a gentleman friend,
a kindred spirit, himself over ninety.
Some at their retirement center
called him her boyfriend.

To older sister Gertrude, this was all
most unseemly. When Gertrude learned
that her wayward sibling planned
a cruise with this man, she intoned,
So—you'll be on a boat together.
Will you share a stateroom?

Suspense her game, Wanda paused
for more than a few beats.
Nooooo, she finally exhaled.

You might as well, steamed Gertrude,
Your reputation is already ruined.

Inhaling this time, Wanda replied,
Oh, do you really think so?

The Day She Had the Last Word

At a cafe, well into a long marriage,
they shared a jumbo, too-hot coffee.
To cool the brew, he poured it
from one cup to another, held aloft
over the not-asbestos napkin in his lap.

Be careful, she said, *It's scalding.*
He stayed on course.

Be the agent of your own doom!
She cried, with no small heat.
His instant reply,
last lines from *Paradise Lost:*
And with retorted scorn,
his back he turn'd
on those proud towers
to swift destruction doom'd.

Right, she aspirated.
But we both know
who'll fetch the band-aids
and burn cream.

VII

BOUQUETS

Song of a Girl Knitting

by Rosine Vance Turner, Ithaca, New York,
1959

I'm knitting him a sweater of soft wool
the color of whole wheat, or winter trees,
lavender brown in the distance, as one sees
them from the fireside when the woodbox is full.
He'd wish I wouldn't, if he found me out,
for all that is creative in me goes
into the docile stitches, and I know
he'd have me read or write, and be about
some worthier cause: time is so short and dear.
But I won't tell him and he'll never guess
the hours in it, and if he should press to know
I'll laugh and say, *oh years and years!*
What joy to think of him, all unaware,
enfolded as by love in this my care.

Tribute

for Melanie

You seem the classic
California girl—born there, tall,
slim, graceful as a dancer.
A model? Actress? No.

A stoic warrior heart beats within
your blue flight suit.
Weeks of boot camp gave you
that confident stride.

Still in adolescence, you
entered the world's dark heart
on that March day, part of the air cover
as convoys marched
over the border into Iraq.

Before you flew Black Hawks,
you donned that bulky suit, strode in the dust
to disarm roadside bombs, reached in
with your slender fingers, found the wires.

Later, you flew bomb squads into the minefields.
Soldiers returned with you. Some did not.
Sometimes your strafed craft barely landed at base
before falling apart.
Now, after twelve years and four deployments
to Iraq, Pakistan, and Afghanistan,
you are a civilian. Still flying,
you take patients from remote areas,
land on the hospital roof.

This was not your world at eighteen.
Your youth lies stillborn
in the sand and blood of desert lands.
Your nightscape shadows
are alien and ugly. Your band of brothers?
Scattered, wounded, blown up.

Today you say,
I don't fit in here.
I belong with my brothers.

In all ways but one,
you are with them still.

From Forbush's *Birds of Massachusetts,* 1925

for hm, in memoriam

Buffleheads play in white-topped surf,
perfectly at home,
not in the least inconvenienced
by foaming surge,
raging wind, or stinging cold.
Cheerful, happy, and contented,
intent only on food to help withstand
the cold and stress of winter
on a wave-beaten coast.

So too, the lilies of the field,
who do, however, enjoy
a milder climate.

Thank you to Edward H. Forbush. Love and gratitude to Hugh and Barbara MacMahon, hearty coastal New Englanders who, for a few winters, tried Florida.

I Look On In Wonder

for jrg

You absorbed early blows
sufficient to crush,
bore burdens unfit
for young shoulders.

You knelt, over the years,
seven times
by my reckoning,
sprinkled earth,
sprigs of violets,
arose, and went forth
unsteadily,
yet unbowed,
grace assured.

Rooftop

Fall
The moon glows faint over the East River,
a pale sliver visible to visitors
who lean out too far
over the tenth-floor parapet.

At this hour and height
horns, voices, sirens are muffled,
the garden quiet.
Leafy, trellised, the akebia vine
retreats, prepares for winter—
a more alpine climate here
than below.

Bright floral colors fade now,
frost having taken their charms, their cheer.
Figs, pomegranates, apples lie wrinkled,
decaying on rubber tiles that pass for earth
on the tenth floor.

With grave hope the garden comes to rest
in this, its first year, expecting
a mild burden of wind and snow.
What will survive
should raging gales attack?

Garden, Gone

Summer I
The decade's fiercest winter
left the garden intact—
no hint that nature's wrath
would not be its ruin.

When a country gardener moves away,
leaves his land to fate, or indifferent care,
plants cling to life. Tomatoes reseed,
bear fruit in July. Lilies untended gild
the hillside, asters purple the meadow.
Neglect, time, drought take others—
nature decides.

When a roof-top gardener moves,
his garden, so carefully created,
is not abandoned—
it is torn apart, dismantled.

New residents have other plans.

Six muscular men rip from planters
apple and fig trees, blueberry bushes,
shrubs, gourd-bearing vines, radiant perennials.

Sweltering under a summer sun,
they haul away a hundred bags—
no longer fertile earth, merely dirt.
Last, the planters—
down the elevator, loaded on trucks.

Sad, undignified travel
for a young family, so varied
in size, shape, temperament, yet united
in cause, service to green and golden hue,
apple, berry, rose-violet, red and blue.

Garden gone: a flat, clean-swept roof,
final clumps of earth pulverized
by a power hose.

Summer II
Bereft, the city-dweller might look to
those who drive his garden away.
Will they divide among neighbors
the planters, akebia vines, fruit trees,
the parsley, basil, and lemon balm?
The trellis?

Perhaps a deck in Queens, a fire escape
in the Bronx, a backyard in Brooklyn,
will soon welcome, plant anew
the brave exalted few
born atop a roof.

For Gene Kelly

Singing, rain—*what a glorious*
feeling! And dancing in the rain,
your sublime smile
a confection, you splash
ankle-deep in charmed puddles, swing
into history on a lamp-post, spin
an umbrella—your engine, your sail.

Years pass, wars are fought,
children grow, and trees.
You, still airborne on eternal breeze.
We watch your jumping joy
and recall anew
all we have forgotten
about dance, about rain
and young love.

Only in New York

The young Dominican monk's white robe
brushed his sandals
as he stepped from the escalator
onto the crowded subway platform.

Two skeptics engaged him in small talk,
then requested, with faint mockery,
that he offer in that place,
a sample of Gregorian chant.

His strong tenor startled the rush-hour crowd.

Fifty feet above them, six men in white
joined their voices to his, descending slowly,
morning mist rolling down a hillside,
sacred tones ringing through stone arches
in that dim corridor.

From Time Beyond

for Saniya

You had recently birthed a daughter
and I a son, when you, Saniya, said,
You know we were sisters many lifetimes ago.
If so, yours was the older soul, heir
to desert wisdom of Arabs ancient
and holy, as with such grace
did you over time reveal to me
much of what we needed
to know
to live the lives we needed
to live.

And The Stars Were Shining

The clarinet sings
as Tosca's doomed tenor,
high on a rampart,
begins a new ascent.
A distant drum—
summer thunder
warning,
and a wild cry
pierces the sky.

*Puccini's character Cavaradossi sings the great aria E Lucevan
le Stelle, fondly recalling, in the face of death, days of love and
joy with Tosca.*

Iron Girl

for Kathryn

Striding jubilantly from a two point
four mile ocean swim, she calls out,
I could stay in all day.
The morning still young.

Dripping wet, rush to cycle,
warm Florida air on cool skin,
over one hundred miles to pedal.
Still exhilarated.

Darkness descends on runners,
their twenty-six miles on foot,
finishing fifteen hours of Ironman.
Speechless. Exuding exuberance.

And exultation. She had
grown strong while young,
turned strength out
to the world—roads, oceans,
conquering each in turn.

Valentine

for Kevin

A classmate in your second grade room, timid
Carley spoke, moved slowly, was shunned.

A field trip—Carley held fast all day
to your chaperone mother,
while you raced happily
with boisterous boys.
Later, urged to be kind to Carley,
you looked away, a seven-year-old after all.

Days later you came home sullen, sad,
burst into choking tears:
I tried, gave Carley a Valentine, she
showed everyone, boys teased me all day,
I'll never go back . . .
Your mother, never prouder,
melted for shy Carley
and her brave boy.

Your large heart opened young,
learned the price could be steep,
but you would ever after offer shelter
to those small and in need.

Reader

for Colin

Nesting on the parental bed,
around which family prayers were said,
we read and read, flying through
Narnia and Prydain; Gurgy half-boy, pure joy
with his rhyming and climbing.

Soon you read them all yourself, and more.
One day in mid read-aloud of Sherlock Holmes,
you stopped your father to ask,
Are you alright Dad?
You look crestfallen.
By then we knew much
about your heart, soul, and
expanding vocabulary.

Retail Caper

for Christian

A simple business model:
young entrepreneur,
borrowed capital, reliable supplier.
Captive audience, sell below retail.

Eight-hundred dollars in a few months,
a fortune for a nine-year-old
selling candy on the school bus.

Alas, bureaucracy scorns success.
Illegal! cried the principal,
hauling in the tycoon
of fourth grade. *It stops now,*
or I throw the book at you!

Later that day:
Mom, Dad, I can see why
they'd stop my business,
but why would the principal
throw a book at me?

Christian's Music

for cwm

Piano keyboard being too high,
on tiptoe, you reach up, touch keys,
knowing somehow,
these notes await you.

You play several keys, call out,
Come hear sounds! So splendid
are they to you, at two.

At three, you play melodies,
find them in memory,
or the moment.
The left hand follows in time,
sealing the partnership.

Ever after, our house fills
with the sounding joy
of your music.

Hope and Heart

for Hope

You contain your name.
Each plan just out of reach,
no silver spoon in sight.
And yet. While raising your beloved son—
a second degree, years of teaching
in a place frightening to grown men—
the seventh grade classroom.

In time, something subdued arose.
Hope, courage too, again your allies.
A new degree, hard-won. Now,
the writer you always were,
talents honed by Hope with heart.

Friend for Life

for my sister, Diane

Born a beauty, also virtuous,
a convergence to celebrate.
A certain feistiness, deployed
for causes beyond your own—
injustice forestalled, unkindness abated.

All practice for raising a quartet of sons.
Tumult typical—arms fractured, heads bloodied,
careening off to clinics, bodies mended,
the crucible steeling your nerves.
Four fine men now.

Then, a daughter! Surrounded, mother and
daughter endure, learn mercy, patience,
both wise before your time.

Brotherly Love

for Richard

Still full of life after a full life, you radiate
fellow-feeling, camaraderie.
Making friends—like eating popcorn,
first one, then another—so simple . . .

Which is not to say you discard them
with ease. Loyal always,
You keep friends as you keep
your Harleys, a fine collection
maintained with care, affection.

Early in life you patented
your own brand of folk wisdom—
barn-building, passionate politics,
and motorcycle mania.
Long may your sun shine.

Men to Sea

for Bill

In that ivy-clad cloister,
aged buildings amid a sea
of emerald lawns, you write
dozens of pages on T.S. Eliot.

You blink, and are gunnery officer
on the *Noa,* Navy destroyer training
for battle in the Mediterranean.

Three years at sea, breathing the life,
lore, salt air. Next, five years,
more ivy, poring over alien pages
for yet another world. The sea now
lingers only within.

Another blink: a family, a college
to manage, build. Another campus,
one task follows another, and you
still the Irish lad whose father crossed
an ocean in search of life
for his sons.

Now, you hold dear: children, Newman's words,
walks at dawn, an occasional fine wine, music always,
and Mass in the morning.

VIII

GRANDCHILDREN

Grand Parenting

for Claire

How to portray the firstborn
of our own first child?
Ah, the rapid descent
into rosy sentiment.

Such a beautiful baby!
Everyone laughs—
they've heard it all before.

Her passage to life brought pain and blood.
Like royalty, she changed
a place in the world,
bestowed titles at birth:
ordinary mortals became mother, father,
uncle, aunt, grandfolk.

Tender skin, glow of sunrise,
lips shaped like early violets,
a rose-petal tongue.

No further words.
Gaze on perfection
and in silence, rejoice
            rejoice
                rejoice . . .

Claire at Three, Future Debater, Asks

What's a brunch?
A meal, like breakfast, but in late morning.

But what does it do?
Well, we all sit down and . . .

No, no, what does it dooooooo?
(All are baffled and bewildered)

You know, like when it steals Christmas?

Small Miracles

Wind-whippers wipe windshields
in the rain.
Loshclosh and soap send grime
down the drain.
Alla Fadda who art in heaven,
begins the praying.

Words arrive, day by day, keys
to laughter, secrets, stories.
To trouble, kindness, care;
the need to listen
and beware.

Loshclosh was Claire's first attempt to say washcloth.

Do Not Discard Your Ticket Stubs

A strong message told
by the Imax screen.
In the car later, I asked my husband—
he is after all, older than I—
How long do we need to keep our stubs?
Five years, he shot back.

Hearing the exchange, Claire
in back rolled her eyes, unfurled
a six-year-old's sardonic smile.

Well, I asked, *How long do you think?*

Mischief backfired—she turned serious, worried,
began to consider the issue. She is conscientious,
would never, when older, remove
the Do Not Remove tag from a mattress.

I interrupted her silent deliberations:
Do you think Grandpa was serious,
or just being silly?

Relief in a flash, bright sunlight on her open, tender face.
Oh silly,
definitely silly.

Sebastian at Three

You are our little wild man,
our yellow-haired Russian boy.

Your sly smile tells us
you know what is naughty.
Your slender frame belies
the mighty force within.

Sebastian's great-grandmother emigrated from Ukraine.

Clearly You Will Conquer Mountains

for Sebastian

When very young, you loved hard surfaces,
steel, cement, stone—no stuffed bears for you.

On walks, I look for AC units stuck to houses,
and of course, garbage trucks.
The men know me.

At the site, tall cranes rear their clamping jaws
three stories into the sky. Tractors' massive treads
lumber across fresh red earth. Wrecking crews
destroy everything. Enchanted,
you beg
to stay another hour.

That's when I'm happiest
of the whole day.

Boat Race

In a cerulean sky, the sun hides
behind floating crowds of cotton clouds.
Sailing fans stand on a Florida pier,
cheering on the straggler skiff,
last in a field of eight. A stiff wind
fills gleaming sails, sends all a-skim.

At the final turn, straggler's sails
meet a fierce gust; she takes on water,
all but capsizes. At the moment of peril,
bright sun emerges, dripping diamonds
into the dark sea.

Happy omen? No, but the brave boat
rights herself—*I think I can*—
takes a fine breeze for the straight-away,
finishes last—dignity intact—
her captain beaming.

The young skipper reaches down
into the bay,
gently lifts his ten-pound boat,
dries her off, stows her away,
to race again another day.

Ryder at Seven

He can't quite make change
or tie his shoes.
Can tell time—a little.
Loves his dog and stuffed animals.

But with violin in hand
small fingers fly,
his bow plying each string
through song after song.

He hears music once, twice—
fingering, bowing begin.
Notes, rhythm, melodies come forth,
bidden from unseen sources.

Now, Bach or Mozart,
then, fiddle style—
"Boil them Cabbage Down."

How does a boy, a family
manage sacred mystery, a gift
beyond all understanding?

This is only the beginning.

Castle of Many Kings

for Ryder

Trim staircase slides out of sight
hidden in the wooden castle where
drawbridge spans blue moat.
Fearsome portcullis drops down:
entry denied to fierce plastic knights
and green dragon. Four-inch dungeon
holds the captured. Small queen
peers from tall turret.

Fifty years ago, three brothers
and a sister held court, boldly
deployed swords, soldiers, dragon—
until wider lives beckoned.

Thirty years pass. Grandparent
grounds crew makes all gleam
for a new reign: brother and sister
(heirs of the first queen)
preside happy, supreme.

And then it was your turn, single boy.
At two, you bring Lego people to the castle.
Jenga blocks are sentries, battalions, beds
or barriers. Soon Star Wars arrives, fills
little lives with battle and bomb,
yellow 'copter and black rocket ship.

You are king for a decade,
as medieval fantasy melts
and merges into modern.

In time, castle life calms, king's
visits are few—other worlds call.
Your anchor still pulls—some days,
old stories play again as new.

Then you move; a thousand miles
between boy and moment.
Royal crew performs
its ancient ritual—corners and
corridors cleaned, covered
with soft cloth, tucked
safely away.

Years pass. Returning,
you retrace time, hours.
Now your children find towers,
moat, and secret room.

No thought of doom!
Horses dash, soldiers clash,
swords flashing,
rush the stair,
scale palisade, barricade,
find green dragon
in king's lair!

Untimely Invasions

Captain, O Captain
of industry. Titan
of Wall Street,
not so long ago.

Now your desk at home
is approached, spade in hand,
as for an archaeological dig.
Layers of Legos tell the tale.
Piled on stock analyses, here
a copy of *Goodnight Moon,*
there *Winnie the Pooh,*
and the *Wall Street Journal.*

An errant rubber ducky waddles in,
wet from resident grandson's bath,
little droplets gradually soak through all.

Storytime

for all grandchildren

The moon's a golden galleon,
the sky all blue and foam.
You are captain, I am crew
as we sail through tales
of derring and do.

And when it's time
to leave our moonboat,
we plunge laughing down
and down through cloudy deep,
landing gently in your soft bed,
sound asleep.

Written with Bill Moran.

IX

EVENING

Anniversary Tale

Survival Tools II

The plane, airborne
for twenty minutes.
The man and woman,
seat belts tight, shoes loose,
deep into their books
and the Friday newspapers.

She, nudging him, offered a set-up line.
When we arrive I will know
about all the plays and films opening
this weekend, and you will not.
He, barely looking up from a book she
judged too heavy for travel, murmured,
I fervently hope so.

Thus did they survive fifty years
of marriage, numerous children,
and his retirement.

Tables Periodic

Fifty years since the couple
dined with plates on laps.
Soon, a step up—card table.
Then an attic find, barely
sufficient: two children
in high chairs, two more at table
atop thick cushions.

Eventually, and for another decade,
family of six around an old oak table,
stripped of its dark stain, a leaf added.

Later still, a small table, no leaves,
seating two, and the occasional visitor.

Around a nearby corner is the day
one will dine alone at a tray table.
For such moments, the French grandmother
had offered timeless advice,
Sufficient to the day is the evil thereof.
The Talmud agrees: *Sufficient is the trouble of the hour.*
We will table the issue for another day . . .

*What she really said was: Suffisant pour le jour est le mal de celui-
ci. By then I'd lost most of my French, alas, and had to use Google
to translate.*

Claustrophobic Clutter

Four and twenty blackbirds
baked in many pies.
All flew out and pecked
at her eyes.
A new crowd of crows
aimed at her nose.

Diving birds croaked in her ears,
too much, too much, too much
down all the long years.

Waking, rid of crows
and crowds, dazed at first,
she soon knew:
bad turns to worse.

Dying Condition

It's time I put this house
in a dying condition.
That would be my dying,
mind you,
not the house.
That means you
who have taken up space
all these years
must prove your worth.
If you demonstrate,
and quickly, your true
indispensability, you stay,
lodged in a file labeled in large font:

Homemade Mother's Day Cards
Letters to Cherish
Recipes for 2 That Take 4 Minutes
Books to Read Again (or not)
Dozens of files . . .
But if you fail to meet
my idiosyncratic tests, Out!

To the ash-heap of my own history,
you brittle brown-edged newspaper clippings,
you torn and faded photographs,
you mouse-nibbled textbooks, Out!
Out! Out!

But first, let me look at you,
just one more time.

Intervention, Anyone?

They call it a rush—
insolent chemicals presuming
to flood the mind, commanding it
to float on a cloud of delight.

Favorite sport: Scrolling Down.
Mighty cursor-trained fingertip
engages an arrow, brings on
the world as carnival—news,
jokes, games—all equal,
messages, memes, movies, music,
meetings, virtual this, Zooming that.
Numbing, *delicious* onslaught.

Turn it off! Calls a tiny inner voice.
Ignored.
More! Screams greedy,
needy triumphant addicted
Self.

HELP!

They Call It Discomfort

You are a constant presence.
Your loyalty is touching,
but you are not a friend.

I may have adjusted
to your company;
never will I welcome it.

You offer benefits, I'm told—
a spiritual silver lining, dear-won
wisdom of the ages?

Perhaps in time I will
grasp your lessons. Meanwhile,
you *are* an *awful* pain.

Doctor's Diagnosis

Scoliosis
Osteoporosis
Spondylosis
Osteoarthoidosis and
a lovely touch of
Stenosis.

Said patient, *Are you seriosis?*
Yes, he replied, *but*
once we take out your osis,
you'll soon be
super fine and expialid . . .

July

Summer shadows splay
across the road
like spilled ink.

Dog and I breathe,
bathe in fresh dew,
and morning-cool air.

She rolls, I stroll.

Home at last, we say
How fine! and turn,
she to her bowl,
I to my brew.

Kneading New Knees

Her older children, now in their forties,
remember her cheerfully carrying
a toddler under one arm,
and a yearling on the hip,
while pregnant.
She was always the one
to lift, pick up, carry.
They are gradually learning,
as she is, that someday she will be
lifted, picked up, carried.

Imagine a truck
filled with two by fours
tied in packets with rope.
A batch falls off the truck—
their mother arising in the morning.
A second packet falls, scattering
the first like pick-up sticks—
her efforts to walk downstairs.

At last a great force reaches down,
pulls the rope, secures the packet.
The grace of God
helping her to move through the day.

Potions, Creams, Emollients

Dutiful, contrite,
we apply to nature's blight
approved blend and brew,
herbal, earthly, drops of dew.

Yet we lurch on
unamended.
If time were suspended,
wayward skin
defended, would not all
be reclaimed, made right?
Ah, but salves alone
detain not
a single night.

X

LATE EVENING

Turning Eighty

In her eightieth year,
she felt herself crumple,
not crumble, as an old house falls apart,
dropping one brick after another.

No, she crumpled,
as a sheet of newspaper,
prepared for a fire.

The structure gone,
nothing firm, upstanding,
all folded in on itself.

Year Eighty-One

Surprise! A rebirth. Of sorts.
Not according to nature's usual
pattern—cruel, heedless of hopes, plans.

Instead, rejuvenation—relative, of course.
No marathon runs, just a quickening step.
Pain faded, gone. Relief, renewal.
Gifts of a new day, a year.

Who knows what lurks
in the shadows of eighty-two?

Debris

If I knew
what was expected,
what was required
of muddled mortals,
I would seek, at least,
a divestment,
an unjumbling.

Instead, so many
minutes and hours,
rooms and places,
spaces in the mind,
choke with debris.

Spaces Between

Phrases, poems write themselves
in the nightmind.
Reverie, memory, story.
Sleeping, waking—
which are real, which
just intervals in dreamscape?

She never quite knew,
pondering too,
are we daily alert, curious,
or floating on interludes?

So much we never know.
In the end, we know more
and less.

A Moment

The vase of Black-eyed Susans centers
a blue and white checkered cloth,
as filtered morning light plays
on the round table.

Reminders of humble virtues,
domestic order,
and the leafy maples
of a warm southern spring.

In Lockdown

We do not desperately need
a grand ballroom—
all glam and gleam.
Or
church social—write
checks, then ice cream.
Or
formal fetes at home—
linen, silver, flowers.
Or
picnic, rain showers—
tots run to and fro.
Or
diner breakfast—
bad coffee to go.
Or
hot dog stand—
sit on wet grass.
But
off to recycle glass
in plague-month nine.
Toss empties, fondly recall
the beer, the wine.
This lockdown outing is just fine!

No Minor Mercy

We greet the sun
as it fills the room.
Take it as our due—so too,
food, or deep gulps of air
after sea-frolic
with a laughing child.
Nor do we always note
the lesser mercies—
birds that sing, the golden
green flutter of spring.

But to recover, after long years,
one loved yet lost, carries
no small grace, no few tears.

Then all the failed moments
are redeemed and bright.
Arms open wide,
as the room fills with light.

Casablanca: Te Absolvo

If you
had an innocent secret,
would not reveal it
to one you love,
then you too might
have left Humphrey Bogart
waiting for the train
in the rain.

But if your mind were spacious,
could imagine that pain,
you'd know hearts expand,
are capacious.
You would explain and explain.

Such tales tell of our need
to be shriven—and we learn
again and again—that each
in time will be well
and truly
forgiven.

Dearly Departed

To sail away is to be free,
or so it has always
seemed to be.

Those who hold us dear
with silken thread
would keep us near.
Oh, that we were stayed!

Yet horizons beckon.
We sail on alone,
soon to be welcomed,
welcomed home.

ACKNOWLEDGMENTS

O ver the years of writing these poems and stories in verse, I was fortunate to be encouraged by wise, experienced, and generous teachers.

My parents were extraordinary teachers. Born in Brooklyn, New York, into modest circumstances, Ted and Eleanor Baillet combined their major resources—energy and imagination—and moved to Long Island as it shed its farmland past. With strong civic instincts, both Baillets took leadership roles in helping to create a surprisingly cohesive entity from meadows, woodlands, and a large housing tract.

In the context of a nearly idyllic, semi-rural childhood, my brother, sister, and I absorbed the values of our parents, members of the "greatest generation." Their lessons of perseverance, honesty, patriotism, sharing with those in need, planning ahead, commitment to faith and family guided us as we forged our own lives. I will be forever grateful to my parents for the foundation they provided for their children.

Bill Moran, my next great teacher, majored in Lyric and Reflective Poetry at Princeton, then immediately went to sea for three years as a Gunnery Officer for the U.S. Navy, followed by degrees at Harvard Business School and University of Michigan. His grasp of the contrasts between those four worlds, and his successful efforts to balance them thereafter, gave me a way of seeing that I might not otherwise have acquired. Life with Bill Moran has been a continuing education in poetry, history, economics, Navy lore, and vaudeville-style humor.

Evelyn Gill, founder of the International Poetry Review, published my early poetry and stories and remained a valued mentor for the rest of her life.

Elizabeth Sewell, British poet, critic, and novelist, offered fine lessons in life and literature. Ms. Sewell stressed the importance of heeding the call of pre-dawn rumination, my future wellspring.

Brenda Schleunes, founder of the North Carolina Touring Theater Ensemble, taught me to seek tales from the oral tradition, while offering a warm welcome into the world of storytelling and performance. She was a true and generous mentor.

Fred Chappell is widely revered for his extensive body of work, stellar teaching, and vast kindness to fledgling writers. He and his wife Susan were early and reassuring readers of my work. His writing taught me, among many other things, that the zaniest humor can be deployed for high (or low) purpose.

Years earlier, I was deeply influenced by the great South African writer and anti-apartheid activist Alan Paton, who spent two months on our Flint campus. I cherish his only version of the hand-written speech he gave me immediately after the Commencement for which he wrote it. Alan Paton combined great courage, rooted in deep religious convictions, with fearless political activity. For years, he sacrificed the writing he loved for leadership on his country's most urgent issues. He taught me about priorities long before I had choices.

Among many other writers whose work affected me deeply at different times of life are Shakespeare, W. H. Auden, William Butler Yeats, Albert Camus (for *The Plague*), Saul Bellow, George Eliot, Edna St. Vincent Millay, Billy Collins, historians Paul Johnson and Loren Schweninger, essayist Lance Morrow, and economist Thomas Sowell.

Over the years, we lived in New York, Michigan, Massachusetts, and North Carolina, making lasting friendships in each state. But for forty years, home and friends have been in Greensboro, N.C., a beautiful Southern city that is especially welcoming to artists, musicians, and writers. Writers, especially, seem to flourish here.

Friends from various states who offered encouragement at crucial moments include Marilyn Tyler, Mary Jellicorse, Harrell and Ivory Roberts, Stan Jenkins, Steve and Catherine Popell, Saniya and Ted Hamady, Naomi Galbraith, Judith Williams, Betsy McMann, Katherine Wingert, Laurie White, Patsy Kendall, Jim Gutsell, Carolyn Toben, Vivian Lemons, Sally Vasse, Meliwe Nxumalo, and Shih-min L. Wu.

This may be the best place to mention that two of the pieces included here are not my own. "Song of A Girl Knitting" was written by my Cornell University roommate, Rosine Vance Turner (who is still married to the object of her poetic affections). I treasure this sonnet and have saved the original typewritten page for sixty years. Rosine is out of reach now, but I wish to honor her by including her lovely poem in this collection.

The list poem "I Hate (not necessarily in that order)" was written by our son Kevin at age twelve. I include it (with his permission) because its quirky, hyper-aware sensibility remains entertaining and revealing.

I am indebted to fellow members of the New Garden Poetry Group for their candid critiques over the years. The late Judith Behar, lawyer and poet extraordinaire, left no poem unscathed by her disciplined and penetrating appraisals. But, oh, did we learn!

I greatly appreciated editorial notations and steely-eyed appraisals by early reviewers of the manuscript: Jing Tsu, Catherine Mattingly, Walter Beale, Jane Gutsell, Kathryn Troxler, Connie Ralston, Laura Lomax, and Keith Cushman. Their insights were astute and astringent.

Ioana Galu, whose first language is Romanian, read my earlier book with the same exquisite care that she applies to her music, noting minor details and little hidden jokes that I'd forgotten. Few writers encounter so thorough a reader as this noted violinist and radiant child of then-Communist Romania. I was deeply moved and grateful for the level of attention Ioana gave to my work.

Scott Davis was facilitator, advisor, editor, designer, guide—without whose expertise, patience, and judgment I would still be wandering in a technological wilderness. My gratitude is unbounded!

Also to our extended family, thank you for moral and material support at important times: Tim and Deneen Moore, Vivian Bussey, Daniela Cabezas Pena, Omaira Rojas, Bill Grace, Marissa and Jamie Pipkin, Karen Cramar, and the incomparable nourisher, Santa Touria—Touria Rimawi.

It would take a long page to list the many ways Tim Moore has for twenty-five years kept together for us house and land, head and heart. We will never forget his courage, kindness, many skills, and loving spirit.

Much love and appreciation goes to my family: daughter Kathryn Moran and her children, Sebastian and Claire Silberman; sons Christian Moran, Colin Moran, Kevin Moran, and his son Ryder Moran; Ryder's mother Hope Cammerari; siblings Diane Baillet Meakem, Richard and Carole Baillet.

Thank you all for the life I have been blessed to live with you and for being the beloved subjects of my stories and poems.

Most of all, I am everlastingly grateful to my husband Bill Moran, patient husband of fifty-eight years, without whose love, support, piercing wit, and delight in language, this work would not have just happened.

ABOUT THE AUTHOR

Barbara Baillet Moran, husband Bill, and their children led a quiet life in Stony Brook, New York, until Bill was offered the job of Chancellor of the University of Michigan campus in Flint, Michigan. His mandate was to build a new campus. He was thirty-nine years old and, in eight years, did just that.

Barbara's life changed overnight. At thirty-three and with four children under six, she began a new life. For the next twenty-three years, the couple would live and raise their children in two campus homes. The writing she had always pursued was hampered by constant commotion. And happily so, she is quick to add.

Having previously entertained only friends at home, Barbara now worked with University staff to plan receptions for hundreds of strangers, formal dinners for thirty, and dozens of smaller events. Guest lists included students, alumni, office staff, faculty, indoor and outdoor maintenance staff, local and state politicians, people distinguished in fields from academia to the arts, science, and journalism. President Gerald Ford and twenty-six Secret Service agents came for lunch one afternoon.

During midlife, much of Barbara's writing became more specific as she delved into children's literature, storytelling, and the oral tradition. Inspired by the wide range of people who visited the chancellor's residence in Flint, and later, the University of North Carolina at Greensboro, she gradually focused on the field of oral history and personal stories.

Barbara's first book, *Voices of the Silent Generation*, subtitled *Strong Women Tell Their Stories* (2006), consisted of a brief history of the 1950s and oral histories of women who, in an era that was inhospitable to women, had forged successful professional and personal lives. The book attempted to answer the question, "How did that happen?" The first edition sold out in a few months.

With retirement, a quieter life allowed memories to surface. A new way of writing emerged, and for the last three decades, Barbara has written and published poetry, stories, and essays in a variety of periodicals and anthologies. *What Just Happened* is her first book of poetry and stories in verse.